THIS WALKER BOOK BELONGS TO:

_____

_____

_____

For Dad and Patti, in honour of their five 🐖 anniversary
A. P. S. & J. S.

The dogs are for Mum, the rest of the book is for Roy
R. C.

First published 2003 by Walker Books Ltd
87 Vauxhall Walk, London SE11 5HJ

This edition published 2004

15 17 19 20 18 16

Text © 2003 April Pulley Sayre and Jeff Sayre
Illustrations © 2003 Randy Cecil

This book has been typeset in Maiandra

Printed in China

British Library Cataloguing in Publication Data:
a catalogue record for this book is available from the British Library

ISBN 978-1-84428-164-0

www.walker.co.uk

One Is a Snail
Ten Is a Crab

A Counting by Feet Book

April Pulley Sayre and Jeff Sayre

illustrated by Randy Cecil

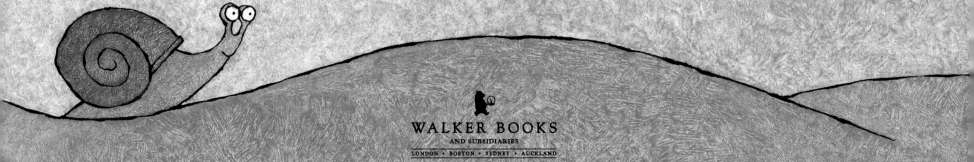

WALKER BOOKS
AND SUBSIDIARIES
LONDON · BOSTON · SYDNEY · AUCKLAND

1 is a snail.

(This is a snail's foot.)

2 is a person.

3 is a person and a snail.

5 is a dog and a snail.

6 is an insect.

8

is a spider.

9 is a spider and a snail.

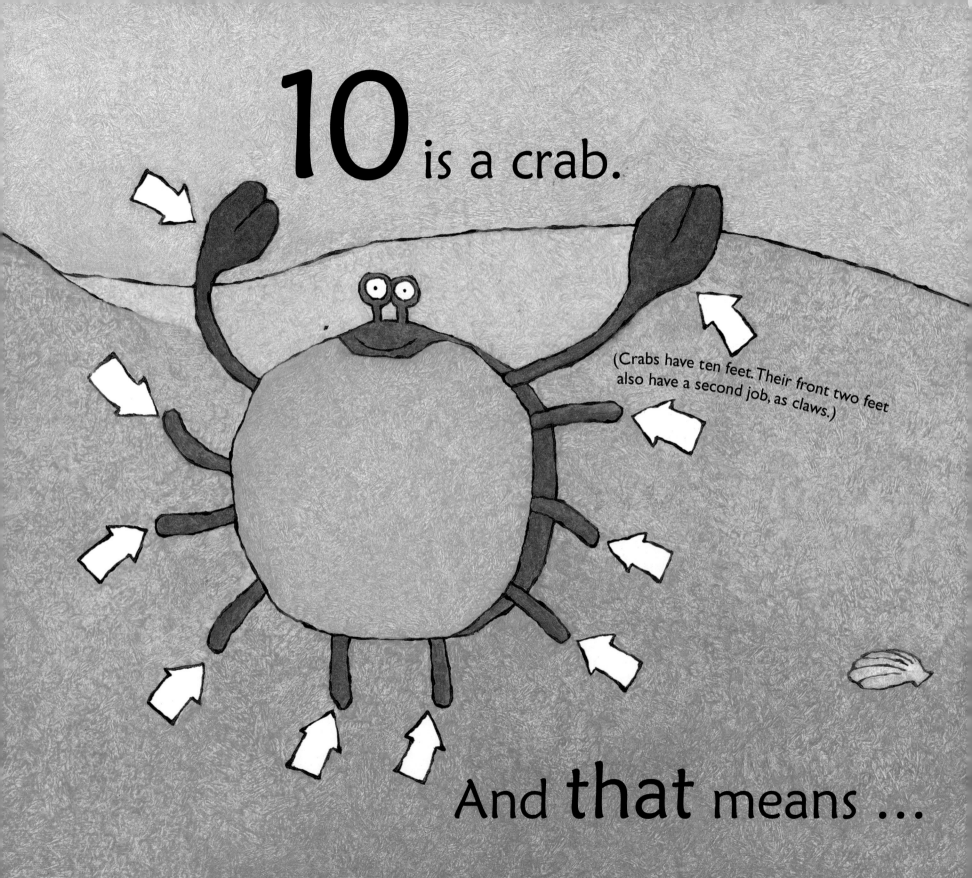

20 is two crabs.

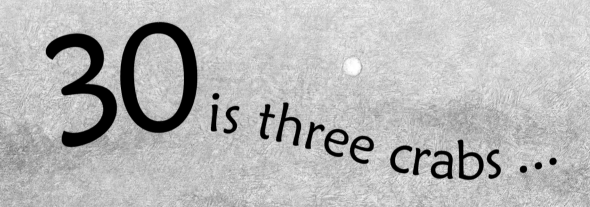

30 is three crabs ...

Or ten people and a crab.

or ten dogs.

50 is five crabs ...

Or ten dogs and a crab.

Or ten insects.

or
ten insects and a crab.

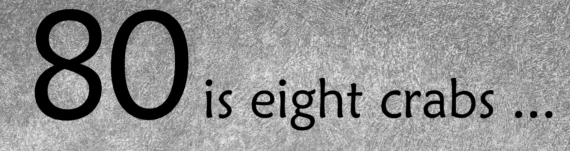

80 is eight crabs ...

Or ten spiders.

90 is nine crabs ...

or
ten spiders and a crab.

So,
100
is ten crabs ...

Or, if you're really counting slowly ...

one hundred snails!